DEDICATION

This book is dedicated to my wife, Sylvia, and my family for believing in me and for supporting my motocross habit over the last fourteen years.

WARNING

Freestyle motocross is an extremely dangerous and sometimes deadly sport. All riders pictured in this book are professionals using proper protective gear under controlled conditions. This book is not and should not serve as an instructional manual, but rather is an explanation of how riders perform insane freestyle motocross moves. Attempting to duplicate any of these maneuvers may be hazardous and/or fatal and is not recommended. Readers are cautioned that individual abilities, motorcycles, terrain, jumps, and riding conditions differ, and due to these unlimited factors beyond the control of the authors and riders quoted in this book, liability is expressly disclaimed. Do not attempt any maneuvers, stunts, or techniques that are beyond your capabilities.

First published in 2002 by MBI Publishing Company, Galtier Plaza, Suite 200, 380 Jackson Street, St. Paul, MN 55101-3885 USA

© Garth Milan, 2002

MBI Publishing Company books are also available at discounts in bulk quantity for industrial or sales-promotional use. For details write to Special Sales Manager at Motorbooks International Wholesalers & Distributors, Galtier Plaza, Suite 200, 380 Jackson Street, St. Paul, MN 55101-3885 USA

Library of Congress Cataloging-in-Publication Data
Milan, Garth
    Freestyle motocross: jump tricks from the pros / Garth Milan.
        p. cm.
    Includes index
    ISBN 0-7603-1184-6 (pbk. : alk. paper)
        1. Motocross. I. Title.

On the front cover: Travis Pastrana

On the frontispiece: Tommy Clowers, Ramona, California

On the title page: Dan Pastor, Ocotilla Wells

On the table of contents : Ronnie Faisst, whip at the Mulisha Compound in Temecula

On the index page: Jeff Tilton, whip at Ocotillo Wells

On the back cover: *Inset:* Clifford Adoptante, Shaolin Bar Hop at Philadelphia, PA *Main:* Dustin Miller, Whipped Double Nac at Philadelphia, PA

Edited by Sara Perfetti
Layout by Liz Tufte

Printed in China

FREESTYLE MOTOCROSS 2
AIR SICKNESS
MORE JUMP TRICKS FROM THE PROS

GARTH MILAN

MBI Publishing Company

CONTENTS

Acknowledgments 7

Foreword by
Jeff Tilton 8

Bike Preparation 10

Rider Bios 16

Kiss of Death
with Mike Jones 24

Hart Attack
Double Seat Grab
with Trevor Vines 30

Whip
with Jeremy Stenberg 36

Hart Attack
Look Back
with Tommy Clowers 42

Shaolin Bar Hop
with Ronnie Faisst 48

Nothing
with Jeff Tilton 54

One-Handed
Seat Grab
with Brian Deegan 60

Whipped Double
Nac Nac
with Mike Jones 66

Cat Nac
with Tommy Clowers 72

Indian Air
Double Seat Grab
with Trevor Vines 78

Indian Air Bar Hop
with Ronnie Faisst 84

Double Nac Nac
Reverse Indian Air
with Brian Deegan 90

Scissored Double
Nac Nac
with Mike Jones 96

Backflip
with Carey Hart 102

Photo Gallery 108

Index 127

I would like to thank a handful of people not only for their contributions to this book but also for making my life easier in general. Topping the list is Donn Maeda, who, over the last two years, has become not only a great co-worker, but also a great friend. Brad McDonald and the rest of my colleagues at Ride Publishing also have my utmost respect and appreciation. You guys are great to work with.

Representin' the West Side, professional photographer Simon Cudby gets big ups for his contributions.

I'd like to thank Lee Klancher from MBI Publishing Company for providing me with the opportunity to publish another book about the best sport in the world.

My family also has my total gratitude for their constant support. If it wasn't for my brother Bret, I would have never been involved in the motocross industry in the first place. My parents have also been instrumental in my success, constantly supporting me in whatever I decide to do.

Last but not least, special thanks are also extended to the riders who contributed so much to the production of this book: Tommy Clowers, Brian Deegan, Ronnie Faisst, Trevor Vines, Mike Jones, Jeff Tilton, and Jeremy Stenberg.

— Garth Milan

by Jeff Tilton

When I entered my first freestyle contest back in 1998 in Tacoma, Washington, I laughed at the whole idea of just going out and jumping my motorcycle for the fans. I was so used to the grind of racing that it was hard to take a step back and just have fun and put on a show.

Once I got out onto the track, I was surprised at how much I enjoyed the event. I didn't have to go out and be the fastest person on the track, I didn't have to have the fastest bike, and I didn't have to go out and take out my buddy in the last corner to try and qualify. In freestyle, we just go out on the

course by ourselves and try to be the biggest show off. I loved it and I haven't looked back since.

Since that fateful day at the Tacoma Dome in 1998, freestyle motocross has become one of the biggest action sports in the world. Led by the X Games, the tricks have gone from sick to insane. There are so many great riders pushing each other to be the best that just about every weekend a new trick or a new variation is executed. I think it's awesome!

Many people want to know if the sport will continue to grow, if new tricks will be created, and if new kids will take over. I say yes, yes, and yes. Every weekend the contests are selling out all over the country. The new people riding the contests are so hungry to be the best that they really push the envelope. There will be more and more competitive events and demos where you can come watch us ride. Every single one of us will be trying to learn new tricks to step the sport up to the next level. And when we aren't out riding events, we're normally out in the desert trying new tricks, freeriding, and being filmed for videos and magazines.

What does this all mean? It means that if you are a fan of freestyle motocross, you should be stoked. Our sport's exposure is on the rise. You can see us in videos, at demos, at freestyle events, at the X Games, on television, in magazines, and in books.

This brings me to this book. Whether you're an up-and-coming rider or just a casual fan who enjoys watching what we do, I think you'll enjoy it. Garth Milan is one of the premiere freestyle motocross photographers and has been involved with the sport since it started. His photos are epic and, in this book, he explains how the best freestyle riders in the world pull off the latest tricks.

Good luck, and I hope the book inspires each and every one of you to get out and ride!

As freestyle motocross has evolved, the riders have adapted motocross bikes to help them pull off tricks. The most popular bikes for freestyle tricks are 250-cc two-stroke motocross machines. The 250s are light and easy enough to throw around but powerful enough to clear 90- and 100-foot jumps without much space for acceleration.

A few riders prefer the lighter and more maneuverable 125-cc machines, including freestyle guru Travis Pastrana. A new wave of performance four-strokes such as the YZ426F and the CRF450R offer riders a viable alternative to two-stokes, but these bikes are less popular with the pros due to the heavier engine weight inherent in the valve-and-cam engine design.

Trevor Vines' factory Yamaha YZ25 is as trick as they come. The large skin on the side of his bike acts like a billboard to showcase his sponsors and also makes his machine easily identifiable.

Cutouts like these in the side panels aid Vines in his seat grab variations. Vines' YZ250 also sports a custom grab handle that attaches with the seat bolts. He uses this extra handle for Indian Air Seat Grabs and also to add more variations to his trick list.

The modifications pros make to their bikes range from small and inconspicuous to completely radical. Many of the changes are "homemade" and done in people's garages, a combination of ingenuity and necessity that has evolved continually based on the needs of specific tricks.

Purchased modifications or professionally performed mods include many of the same things that are offered to beef up motocross racing bikes. Engine and suspension hop-ups offered by aftermarket companies such as Pro Circuit and FMF are among the most common mods. For freestylers, suspension work is the most important of these modifications.

Stock suspension is much too soft for competition and can bottom out on freestyle's steep take-off ramps and hard landings. To safely clear a 90-foot jump common in any freestyle competition, the suspension is revalved and stiffer springs are installed. The stiffer springs are much less dangerous for the rider on both takeoffs and landings.

Engine enhancements aren't as necessary as suspension work,

but are still pretty common and can be critical for clearing big gaps. A variety of engine modifications are common. The most popular are pipe replacement and cylinder porting, both of which change the powerband and delivery. Gearing remains stock for the most part, and power is shifted toward the bottom end and midrange.

Riders also modify the ergonomics of their bikes. This is a typical custom modification generally done at home and to suit the taste of the rider.

Because of the unusually hard landings that freestyle bikes endure, many riders replace their stock spokes with thicker spokes attached to aftermarket hubs. The wide spokes in the front wheel of Trevor's bike are the same size as stock rear spokes to prevent the wheel from blowing out after a hard landing. Trevor's aftermarket front disc brake is also much larger than the stock unit, providing the bike with more stopping power. This is a must for tight courses where the rider has little room to slow his bike down.

Crossbar-less handlebars are the only way to go on freestyle bikes. They allow riders to pull tricks like the Bar Hop without having to worry about catching their feet or legs on the crossbar. Also pictured here are Trevor's forks, which contain heavier springs and stiffer valving to help him out on hard landings.

Behind Vines' plastic side skins lies a heavily modified 250-cc two-stroke engine. An FMF pipe combines with a special carburetor and ported cylinder to deliver maximum power to the motor, which is essential in small arenas where there isn't much room to gain speed for jumps.

Seat foam cutting is one of the most common things that riders do to customize their machines. This involves removing the seat from the bike, taking off the seat cover, and shaving down the foam. The height of the seat is substantially lower after the seat cover is back on and the seat is reinstalled on the bike. This is helpful for tricks such as can-cans, double can-cans, and pendulums, all of which require the rider to raise his legs up and over the saddle. With the seat even an inch lower than stock, it is much easier for a rider's boots to clear it without getting hung up and causing a crash. Seat grabs are also a lot easier with a lowered seat.

Some competitors install taller and/or wider footpegs. The combination of the shaved seat foam and the taller, wider pegs provides a better platform to stand on. It's also a much smaller area for the rider's feet to clear. Pastrana has taken this concept to an even further degree by installing a "dry brake"-style gas tank. Off-road riders commonly use these tanks for quick tank fills. For Pastrana, though, it does a different job. The dry brake gas system eliminates the bulky gas

cap found on a stock bike. This means that he has one less thing to worry about catching his feet on.

Another trick that freestylers have borrowed from off-road riders is the use of steering stabilizers. Landings become much more stable and safe with stabilizers, and they are especially helpful for no-hander-landers. Without a steering stabilizer, the front end can easily get out of control even if the rider lands just slightly sideways.

Another popular alteration you'll see in the pits at a freestyle event is side panel cutouts. This customization involves taking off the side number plates and cutting holes in them with a saw. These holes expose the frame; this then allows the rider to grasp the subframe on a variety of seat grab variations.

A similar modification to the side panel cutout is the custom "grab handle" that is found on the machines of riders including Trevor Vines and Travis Pastrana. These grab handles are metal fabrications or rubber handles that attach to the subframe where the rear seat bolts are located. Extending an inch or two above the seat, the grab handle is used in the same manner as the side panel cutout—assisting with seat grabs and Indian Airs (in which the rider's legs are extended behind the motorcycle).

Grab handles are also found on the fronts of bikes, attached to the top triple clamp. The front grab handles are helpful for tricks like rodeos, when a rider needs something to hold onto while in the air in front of the bike.

The modifications and alterations found on freestyle bikes are as unique as they are important. The right bike setup is crucial to freestyle jumping, and can often help make the difference between pulling off a new trick and hitting the ground the hard way. Aftermarket items such as stiffer suspension springs and engine hop-ups including pipes and porting are critical to proper performance, and can help make big jumps safer for the rider. Modifications to freestyle motocross bikes are very important to the rider's performance and also represent the ingenuity of the competitors.

Shaving down his seat foam is one way Trevor Vines prepares his bike for freestyle. A low seat not only makes it easier for a rider to get his leg over the saddle, but it is also easier to grab the cut-out handles in the side panels during tricks like seat grabs.

Trevor Vines

Like several of the other top freestyle riders, Trevor Vines' freestyle saga is a true rags to riches story. In just a few short years, "Trevor From Wherever" went from being a local professional motocross racer who ran a small parts shop on the side to becoming the first freestyler to earn a full factory ride from a major motorcycle manufacturer. Yamaha's sponsorship of Vines in 2000 helped to further legitimize freestyle. This was a really big deal for Vines and also for the sport in general.

Born in Conneaut, Ohio, 29-year-old Trevor Vines has been riding motorcycles since the age of 10. A successful local racer, Trevor made his way through the ranks of the East Coast and by the early 1990s was qualifying for National events in the pro class. In 1994 a severely shattered ankle, along with some stolen bikes, took the wind out of his sails. Vines still loved the sport and wanted to stay involved, so he started a small motorcycle accessories store in his hometown. Although he wasn't racing as seriously as he was before his injury, having a shop kept him on his bike enough so that he still felt comfortable riding.

Vines still wanted to have fun on his bike but didn't want to spend every waking minute training to race. His life was about to take a major turn. Vines still remembers the event that gave him a new career path and a shot at stardom on his dirt bike.

The first time he watched *Crusty Demons of Dirt* changed his life forever. Seeing Mike Metzger and the crew doing

Heel Clickers and Nac Nacs gave Vines the motivation he needed to get serious about riding again. Immediately after watching the famous video, Trevor was on his bike trying to copy the moves he saw. Tricks came easily to Trevor, and it was obvious that he was a natural when it came to jumping. By 1998, Vines sold his business and became a full-time freestyler. He went on the Warp Tour for the summer and also competed in other freestyle events. Trevor made a name for himself not only because he went huge, but also because he spent the early years of his freestyle career aboard a Yamaha YZF400 four-stroke.

The thundering noise distinguished Vines from his competition, and the crowd couldn't get enough of the loud exhaust. He has since switched to a two-stroke 250-cc bike, but people across the country still remember his old four-stroke.

These days, Vines lives the hectic life of a professional athlete. He competes in close to 50 events each year, nearly all of which require travel. Trevor practices whenever he can, rides around on his R1 street bike, and takes care of his house in Riverside, California. Of all the riders on the circuit, Trevor is known as one of the most professional and clean-cut athletes. This, along with his insane riding talents, has helped Vines earn several major outside, corporate sponsors including Yamaha Motor Corporation and Sobe drinks. Trevor is always a crowd favorite and maintains a good attitude no matter what happens at an event.

Ronnie Faisst

To Ronnie Faisst, freestyle motocross is nothing short of a miracle. His life has been turned upside down by it, all because of a risky, last-minute decision he made a few years ago with his friend Brian Deegan.

The 25-year-old from Summer's Point, New Jersey, was in the middle of a struggling professional motocross career when a chance intervention changed his life. While Faisst was staying at Deegan's house (between the Budd's Creek and Southwick Nationals), Deegan recruited him to film for a Moto XXX video. Faisst had a blast. After the filming, Ronnie was so excited about being in a video that he got caught up in all of it, dropped everything, and decided to go back to California with Deegan and become a video star.

In only a few weeks, Faisst's dreams were coming true. Between video shoots he was scheduled to ride with the Warp Tour—he toured the country with several other athletes doing exhibitions. Ever since, his life and career haven't slowed down a bit.

Faisst now lives in Corona, California. He rides and practices nearly every day at the Metal Mulisha Compound in Temecula along with Mulisha friends and teammates Deegan, Jeremy Stenberg, and Tyler Evans. Although Ronnie is a consistent finisher at contests, he really shines at demos or while practicing with his friends. His unique style is characterized by the extension of

his tricks and his amazing flexibility. Ronnie credits his love of the martial arts, which he's been involved in since the age of five, for his extension and flexibility.

Another cross-training activity that Faisst takes advantage of is BMX jumping. Ronnie tries to ride his bicycle a few times a week. In addition to keeping him from burning out, BMX is a great way to stay in shape for the quick freestyle runs he does in competitions, which are usually under 2 minutes. Faisst prefers the short, intense freestyle format compared to the 40-minute motos of outdoor racing, which require much more intense training.

According to Faisst, freestyle has several distinct advantages over motocross racing. The most important is the fairness of the sport. Unlike the elite freestylers, the top factory motocrossers have a huge advantage over their competition because of the bikes they ride and the works parts they receive. In freestyle, bike selection and performance aren't as critical and individual skill is, so the best performance wins. In addition, the costs of freestyle competition are much lower, and because there are fewer competitors, the riders make a better living.

Faisst plans to continue competing in freestyle events for at least ten more years, and future plans include inventing some new tricks and just having fun. Ronnie loves jumping, and as long as he can continue to make a living riding his motorcycle, you can bet that he'll be out jumping with his Mulisha buddies.

Mike Jones

Of all the riders on the professional freestyle circuit, no one has been riding, jumping, or partying as long and hard as "Mad" Mike Jones. The 2001 Winter X Games champion has been a constant innovator and made big waves this year by introducing the Kiss of Death, a move that has been copied by many but perfected by few.

Jonesy got his start in freestyle motocross, like most of the other riders, by racing professional motocross and Supercross. Jones started racing at the age of 15, and continued until just recently, giving him a racing career that spanned almost 19 years. In fact, Jones and his family still live on the grounds of one of the biggest racetracks on the National Motocross circuit: the Steel City

Raceway in Delmont, Pennsylvania.

Although Jones will always love racing dirt bikes, his biggest passion is catching air. In fact, Jones was the first rider to perform in halftime jump shows way back in 1987, when he would perform radical (at that time) tricks like whips and no-handers. He continued to learn tricks whenever he could, and by 1993 he was pulling moves like the no-hander-lander that are still popular today. Jones estimates that by 1994 he had about five or six tricks down, an impressive list for the time. Mad Mike has gone on to compete in nearly every event freestyle has to offer since then, and has racked up several event wins.

In it from the beginning, Jones was one of the original riders to compete at the first freestyle contest in 1998. He finished out the season in second place behind Mike Metzger during his first year of competition in the IFMA's contest series. All those years of racing and getting injured were all he needed to make the decision to become a full-time freerider in the late 1990s, and the last race of his career was a Fastcross event in Italy in 2000.

In addition to a full calendar of contests and demos, Jones has capitalized on his famous name. He has performed in several Supercross halftime jump shows in front of thousands of fans at a time. He's also thrilled thousands more fans when he put on demos at events including the Indianapolis 500, the U.S. Open of Supercross, and contests and jump shows around the world. However, there is no argument that his biggest event win to date was at the 2001 Winter X Games: Jonesy took home the gold at the inaugural contest in Vermont. He used a set of spiked tires to stick to the ground on the takeoff and landing of the Big Air Contest jump, at which he unveiled the Kiss of Death.

At the ripe old age of 35, Mad Mike shows no signs of slowing down. It's nearly a sure bet that whatever contest you go to see in the near future, Jones and his mechanic Kibby will be there getting crazy and going huge.

Brian Deegan

Successful motorcycle riding is not a new concept to 27-year-old Brian Deegan. The Canyon Lake, California, resident has carried this idea throughout his career, both in motocross and Supercross, as well as freestyle riding. In fact, Deegan is

arguably the most successful freestyle competitor out there, with a racing resume as impressive as the Indian Air Superman Seat Grabs that he throws.

Deegan began his motorcycle career at age 8 and was racing by 10. Within a few short years, Brian was already racking up championships, with a multitude of wins at major AMA race events including Ponca City. By 18, Deegan was ready to go pro and made the leap in 1992. Working his way up to the top, Deegan became a major threat both indoors and out. In 1997 he accomplished the biggest dream of any aspiring young racer—he won a Supercross main event. With that victory came plenty of controversy; this only foreshadowed what was to come in his career.

After his win at the first round of the 1997 Supercross series in Los Angeles, Deegan was so excited that he decided to "ghost ride" his bike over the finish line to celebrate the win. The fans screamed and so did the AMA. They labeled the stunt as "dangerous" and fined Deegan $1,000. The fine and lectures didn't discourage Deegan, however, and he continued to score several top-five finishes in the outdoor Nationals later in the year.

Around this time, Deegan began starring in some of the big freestyle motocross videos that were taking the MX community by storm. He became known as one of the top freestyle athletes and competed in many freestyle contests. He soon established himself as a top competitor in freestyle.

With all of the money being pumped into freestyle, Deegan soon found that racing was not the way to go. He discovered that he could make way more money by doing what he really loved— going out and having fun with his friends and freeriding.

Once his freestyle career began to take off, Deegan combined his popularity with that of his friend Larry Linkogle, and the two of them joined together to form the Metal Mulisha. The Mulisha began with the two riders just messing around, writing on their bikes with Magic Markers. From there, they decided to have some stickers made, and T-shirts and hats soon followed. Fans took an immediate liking to the name as well as the image, making the company so

successful that Linkogle and Deegan are barely able to keep up with the constant demand for clothes.

Balancing the Metal Mulisha clothing line with his busy freestyle competition schedule is no easy task for Deegan, but he seems to be doing a pretty good job with both sides of his career. In 2000, Deegan captured the LXD Freestyle World Championship, and in 1999 he proved himself a top rider by earning a second at NBC's inaugural Gravity Games and a third at the ESPN X Games, also in 1999.

Deegan plans to compete for at least five more years, at which time he hopes to have enough money invested to retire and run the Metal Mulisha full time. For now, though, he will continue racking up wins and stirring up controversy on the freestyle circuit. Although the press seems to constantly label him as a "rebel" and expose his dark side, in reality Brian Deegan is a quiet guy who honestly likes to help people. Deegan gained his bad boy reputation simply because he is opposed to the corporate butt-kissing of motocross racing, which he says was his main reason for quitting the professional racing circuit. The black outfit and the spiked shoulder pads are just his way of showing his individuality. Nevertheless, whatever your personal take on him is, it's impossible to argue the fact that Deegan is one of the most talented and hardest working riders out there.

Jeff Tilton

Born and raised in one of the most famous and publicized motocross locations in the world, Jeff Tilton has taken full advantage of his El Cajon Zone (California) roots. Known as one of the best natural terrain riders around, "Full Tilt" spent his youth climbing the cliffs of Palm Avenue and jumping the mudhills at Ocotillo Wells. Jeff has been involved in the sport of freestyle motocross since its inception in 1998, but he's been riding motorcycles for more than half his life.

Tilton began his two-wheeled career at the young age of four, when he started racing BMX at local tracks. After four or five years of amateur competition, Tilt was over the peddling scene and talked his parents into getting him a dirt bike.

the decision to give up his racing goals and become a professional freestyler at the end of 1998. Tilt has been at it ever since and is now a regular competitor at contests around the globe, including the X Games and the Gravity Games.

Quitting racing was an easy decision for Jeff. Although he still misses the satisfaction of winning and the adrenaline rush of battling competitors on the track, Tilt has no regrets. Instead of paying money out of his own pocket to ride his motorcycle, Jeff is now able to support himself by doing what he has always loved: riding his motorcycle.

Tilton is a regular contender in the freestyle scene, but he has recently become a businessman as well. Along with his roommate and best friend Tommy Clowers, Jeff co-produced his first motocross video in 2001. Not only does Tilt throw down huge tricks throughout the video, he also shot several scenes, helped edit it, and finished by marketing it.

Taking full advantage of his BMX experience and skills, Jeff caught on quickly and made his way through the ranks at local tracks. By the age of 16, Jeff was chasing the dream as a full-time professional, qualifying for Supercross main events, and holding down a two-digit national number. Although he was successful at racing, Tilt always loved jumping, and in 1997 he found himself with a new sponsor and his life would change forever.

A member of the newly formed SMP motocross team, Jeff was in the right place at the right time to jump onto the freestyle bandwagon. His sponsor gave him the opportunity to participate in some of the early freestyle contests; Tilt decided to enter and do his best. Although he didn't even know how to do any tricks at first, he had such a blast hitting big jumps and throwing whips for the crowd that he made

Tommy Clowers

With 14 amateur national championships to his credit, Tommy Clowers was deemed by several industry insiders to be the next big star in motocross. Growing up in the heart of the Cajon Zone, young Clowers wasn't short on speed or talent. A Team Green ride and a neighborhood full of scorchers including Rick Johnson, Broc Glover, and Ron Lechien were just a few of the things that led Clowers to set the professional MX circuit on fire.

Several top-five Supercross finishes and a big win at the Anaheim Ultracross in 1992 earned the "Tomcat" an NCY/Yamaha support ride in 1993. Clowers proved to be a frontrunner in the

ultra-competitive West Coast 125-cc series, finishing the 1993 season in fourth place behind Damon Huffman.

Unfortunately, 1994 didn't go as well for Clowers. A badly broken ankle at the Houston Supercross put an end to the seemingly unstoppable momentum Tommy had acquired in the early 1990s, leaving him without a ride for the upcoming season. Clowers didn't give up, and with the support of his parents he struggled through the next few years of racing on a shoestring budget that kept him from the results he had hoped for.

Fast forward to 2001, and Clowers is back on top of his game. The shy young man from San Diego County no longer wonders if he'll have enough money to make it to the next race: instead, he jet-sets around the globe, sports his own website, and boasts a laundry list of some of the most respectable sponsors in the sport. From Red Bull to Alpinestars, Clowers is a hot commodity due to successful performances at key events such as the X Games, where he has taken home two gold medals in a row in the step-up competition. Tommy's domination

in the sport is almost uncontested, and the 29-year-old Ramona resident holds the Guinness Book of World Records number-one spot in the event.

When Tommy's not traveling around the world doing contests and demos, he's practicing his craft at Fudge's jumps. Clowers has earned a deserved reputation as one of the hardest-working athletes on the scene, which he believes has made him so successful in the sport. The Tomcat has invented several new tricks that are now considered staple moves in most riders' runs, including the Hart Attack Look Back, the Cat Walk, and the Cat Nac. Some say his small stature helps him throw his body around in the air, but whatever it is, it's obvious that Tommy is a master of freestyle motocross.

Apart from riding, Tommy's other passion in life is golfing. He and his roommate, Jeff Tilton, live in a golf course community in San Diego County, and Tommy spends every free minute whacking the ball around the 18 holes. Other interests include surfing, snowboarding, and BMX, all of which help keep Tommy from burning out on riding.

Jeremy Stenberg

Considered by many to be one of the sport's best riders and a fan favorite, Jeremy "Twitch" Stenberg is in the sport of freestyle motocross for the reason that most people start riding in the first place: he loves to go out with the boys and catch air.

A member of the Metal Mulisha, the 20-year-old from Santee, California, is all about having fun on his dirt bike and doesn't worry about sucking up to corporate sponsors or presenting a clean image. Instead, Twitch presents himself to the world of freestyle just as he is, a sick and twisted kid who throws some of the cleanest tricks in the business.

Like most of the athletes in the sport, Jeremy got a young start with motorcycles. Stenberg's dad got him into riding not long after he was able to walk, and at age three, Twitch was already cruising his three-wheeler down the street by himself. A year later he got his first bike, a CR60. By 11, Twitch was racing in the 80-cc class, but with marginal results. Wanting to get on a 125-cc machine to improve his performance, Twitch's jump up in bike size was a big boost to his success on the track. Soon he was a top Southern California intermediate, just around the

time when freestyle emerged as a separate sport. In between races, Twitch decided to enter some contests, and after only a few, he was addicted.

Every contest taught him something, and Twitch paid attention to the top riders and which moves they were pulling. He studied them, memorized them, and then went to Palm Avenue to practice them. It wasn't long before Twitch starting getting respectable results in contests, and soon he found himself with enough potential in freestyle to give up racing entirely.

In recent months, however, Twitch has gone back to his roots and rarely even competes in contests. Fed up with biased judging, Twitch prefers to go out with his Mulisha buddies and ride. Learning new tricks on his motorcycle is still Jeremy's favorite thing to do, and he and the other Mulisha riders get together nearly every day for a dusk session at the Mulisha Compound in Temecula.

Twitch likes filming for videos or shooting with photographers for his exposure rather than having to ride contests. When he's out in the hills or on his practice ramps having fun, he steps up the level of riding to an amazing level that shines in the many video parts he has had.

The **Kiss of Death** is one of the most publicized, popular, and downright nuttiest tricks that have been introduced to the freestyle world since the beginning of the sport. First seen at the inaugural ESPN Winter X Games in Vermont, the move helped co-inventor "Mad" Mike Jones take his first gold medal in the one of the most publicized freestyle events in the world.

The trick was developed a few short weeks before the contest at Manny's Yard in Lake Elsinore, California. Mike Jones and Ryan Leyba were preparing for the event when the idea came up for the two to try and kiss their front fender, while at the same time kick their legs off of the footpegs toward the rear of the motorcycle, behind the fender. Jones and Leyba took the extension further and further, each of them trying to best the other's last attempt. By the end of the day, the Kiss of Death was born.

Both Leyba and Jones performed the trick at the 2001 Winter X Games. The trick was the most talked-about new move in freestyle's recent history. So just how difficult is it? Well, even freestyle madman Mike Jones cautions all but the best freeriders in the world to avoid attempting the dangerous maneuver.

Although there are several professional riders who are now pulling the Kiss of Death, the riders who are best known for it are the two co-inventors Mike Jones and Ryan Leyba, freestyle king Travis Pastrana, as well as one of the hottest new faces on the circuit, Jake Windham. In the following sequence, Jones performs the trick at the same place he invented it, at Manny's Yard in Elsinore. Jonesy likes to have plenty of air time to pull the trick, so he recommends at least a 70-foot gap with a fairly steep ramp to allow for maximum "pop."

Jake Windham
Philadephia, PA

Mike Jones explains the
KISS OF DEATH

"**The Kiss** of Death is a really hard trick, so be careful on your first attempt and ease into it. You don't want to be completely upside down or you'll end up on your head. The most dangerous part of the trick is the fact that your bike and body must be pitched at just the right angle. If your bike stays too straight and your body flies too high, you'll jump over the bars. If your bike gets too vertical, you'll wind up looping out and landing on your bike."

"**On this jump,** which is set at about 85 feet, I approach the ramp in third gear, readying myself from the beginning to allow for maximum hang time and extension of the trick. Immediately after hitting the ramp face, I pull up as hard as I can on the bars so that the bike gets vertical. Having your bike get vertical is one of the biggest keys to making the trick look good and get a favorable response from the crowd and the judges."

3 "At the same time that I am pulling up on the bars to get the bike vertical, I also throw myself up and off of the footpegs as high and as quickly as I possibly can. I throw my head back as well, which helps my whole body throw itself back and get into the handstand position. I'm extending my arms because that gets me extended further from the bike and looks better."

4 "Once you're starting to float up with the bike, you need to start concentrating on extension. The trick looks best with all of your limbs straight up and down and the rider as far away from his bike as possible. I've also added a little to the trick since I first performed it, and the Kiss of Death is now performed in two different ways. The original version has the rider kissing the front of his fender with his helmet, whereas the newer version has the rider get as vertical as he can while at the same time looking back. Obviously, the latter adds a degree of difficulty, but it's the one that looks coolest."

5 "When at peak extension, if you are kissing the front fender, you want to have your helmet touching the plastic and your legs floating slightly above your head. If you're doing it the other way, you need to put your helmet's mouthpiece all of the way against your chest, as if you are doing a Hart Attack Look Back. Either way, hold it for as long as you can."

"An important part of pulling the Kiss of Death successfully is to make sure you do the trick in one big motion. This can't be stressed enough: of all of the tricks I do, I concentrate the most on this one to make it a smooth motion. Pull on the bars and float back off of the pegs all at once—don't get jerky or you'll crash."

"Coming down from the Kiss of Death is another big, single motion. Just push off of the handlebars with your arms to bring your body back to level, while at the same time forcing your lower torso down by using your stomach muscles and arms to crunch down and find the pegs. You also wind up pulling on the bars on the way down, which straightens out the bike and keeps you from landing in the loop-out position."

KISS OF DEATH

HART ATTACK
DOUBLE SEAT
GRAB

The **Hart Attack Double Seat Grab** is a trick that requires a combination of two different moves thrown at the same time to make it complete. Tracing the trick's history is as easy as going back to the original Superman, which was later extended to a trick called the Superman Seat Grab. Even more impressive than the Superman itself, this trick was again brought over from the BMX world, but this time it wasn't from Supercross star Jeremy McGrath but rather freestyle rider Carey Hart. From there, the Hart Attack was born. This trick had the rider grab the seat like he did with the Superman Seat Grab, but also kick his legs up in the air and become vertical and upside down on the bike, with his feet pointing toward the sky.

Shortly after that, the Double Seat Grab was born. The Double Seat Grab was similar to the standard Superman Seat Grab, where the rider's feet extended outward, but with the Double Seat Grab, the rider lets go of both sides of the bars and grabs cutouts in the rear number plates. With the body more toward the back of the bike, the rider is able to extend the bike way out in front of him, almost floating behind the machine.

It wasn't until later that Kris "The Rock" Rourke decided to combine the two tricks and make the Hart Attack Double Seat Grab. In this trick, the rider grabs both sides of the cutouts and extends his body back and up, with his feet going above his head at peak extension. Trevor Vines pulls the Hart Attack Double Seat Grab on the following pages. He says that the minimum jump length to do this trick is about 60 feet, but the trick is much easier over an 80- to 90-foot-long jump.

Luke Urek

Philadelphia, PA

Trevor Vines explains the
HART ATTACK DOUBLE SEAT GRAB

1 "Hart Attack Seat Grabs are a lot of fun, but they're way harder to do than regular Hart Attacks or Double Grabs because you have to do both in the same trick. You should make sure that you can do both of these tricks by themselves with no problem before you try to pull a Hart Attack Double Seat Grab. I like to have a 90-foot jump to do them on so that I've got plenty of time to extend them. Hit the jump with enough speed so that you don't have to worry about clearing the gap, and be standing nice and tall."

2 "About five feet in the air, after I've made sure that my bike is going the right way and is not too front-end high or going into an endo, I start to reach back and feel for the grab handle that I have cut into the side of my number plate. My head is looking forward and at the same time I reach for the handle, I begin to take my feet off of the pegs."

"Here, I've found the grab handle, and I'm beginning to get high enough in the air that I feel comfortable to start the extension of my legs. You'll notice that my left hand grabbed the bike first; the reason for this is because that is the hand I use when doing standard Hart Attacks, so it just feels more natural to me. I push my legs back a little before releasing my other leg."

"A helpful hint to extend the trick is to throw the bike way out in front of you, using both arms. Continue holding on tightly to your grab handles, and use both arms to keep the bike nice and stable in the air. You want the front end to be slightly higher than the rear but not too much. The secret to getting the Hart Attack portion of the trick started is to tuck your head into the chest, which will make your legs go up higher behind you."

"This is close to full extension, and once I'm here, I concentrate on holding the trick as long as possible. If you have a good grasp on the handles, you should feel fine in the air. Getting here was easy—after I found the handles, I just snapped my legs and torso out in one motion with my abs and hung on."

6 "After I've held the seat grab out for as long as I possibly can, I begin to get back on the bike. The easiest way to do this is to pull the whole machine back toward your body with both hands. This should all be done in the same motion, but your legs will naturally come back first. You need to have them pretty far forward before you let go of the grab handles, otherwise you might lose your bike in midair."

7 "My feet continue their way toward the pegs, and I now feel confident in the fact that I will be able to make the landing with plenty of time, so I release the grab handles and start to reach for the handlebars. I'm bringing my upper body way forward in an effort to get my weight and inertia toward the front of the bike, and I'm almost back to the grips."

8 "Now my hands are back on the handlebars, and I still have a little bit of hang time before I land, so I'm confident that I will pull the trick smoothly. I get back to a comfortable position on the bike and ready myself for landing."

9 "With a couple of feet to spare before I touch down the wheels, I am completely back on my bike and ready. With jumps that are 90 feet plus, you have to make sure you have enough time to gain complete control of the bike before you land so that you can absorb the shock. Bend your knees and elbows slightly to have a smoother landing, and ride away."

WHIP

Of all the tricks in this book, none are older, cooler, or more classic than the **Whip**. This timeless stunt has been performed for decades in the motocross world, and most people give credit to legendary Belgian Roger DeCoster for performing the first one.

Unlike most modern freestyle tricks, the Whip doesn't require the rider to let go of the bike, although sometimes people throw in variations and kick up a foot or pull a hand off the bar to make the trick look better. Instead, the Whip is performed by the rider turning the bike on the lip of a jump, before even going off of it, which causes the rear end of the bike to swing sideways. In addition to the sideways motion, the bike also gets flat in the air. A perfect Whip has the bike flat in the air, with the engine cases parallel to the ground.

Some of the greats can get the bike tipped over even further, with the frame rails tipping up and the tank tipped down.

Not only do racers perform the move to celebrate a victory, they also whip the bike sideways to set the bike up for a landing. Supercross riders, in particular, use Whips to set up for tight corners after short jump landings. With freestylers, though, the trick is performed solely to entertain the crowd, and freestylers have proven that they can take the trick to the next level. In the following sequence, Twitch performs the trick at the Mulisha Compound in Temecula on a jump that is set at about 85 feet. There really is no minimum length for the jump to do a Whip, but the bigger the jump, the more airtime there is to get upside down!

Dan Pastor
Ocotillo Wells, CA

Jeremy Stenberg explains the
WHIP

1 "I've been doing Whips for years now, and they are some of my favorite tricks because you can do them almost anywhere and they look crip. There is an advantage to doing Whips on ramps, though, because the face of the jump never gets rutted out or slippery, so you can really throw the trick hard off of a ramp."

2 "As I'm approaching the ramp in this sequence, I'm standing up, but I'm in a crouching position so that I can get the most pop from the ramp. I'm in third gear, right in the middle of the powerband and being careful not to overrev the bike. When I hit the ramp, I begin making a big carving motion off of the face of it. Depending on the lip of the jump and how far I want to whip it sideways, I will sometimes start on one side of the ramp at the beginning but launch into the air on the opposite side by the time I hit the end of the ramp. This is because I'm making that big carve, which throws the bike sideways in the air."

"While making the carve up the ramp, be sure that at the end of the motion, you start turning the bike back toward the side you started on. If you forget to do this, your bike will launch off the side of the lip and you won't make the landing ramp. It's basically one big swinging motion, and while you are making the turn back toward the other side of the ramp, you'll automatically be going off of the jump with your wheels on their sidewalls. This will also help your bike to get sideways."

"Once in the air, I immediately begin to lean my body off the side of the bike, bringing it toward the side that my front wheel is on. In this sequence, I am throwing the Whip a little bit late to add more style to the trick, but if you want, you can start bringing the rear wheel around almost immediately off of the lip."

5

"I try to get the bike as horizontal and flat as I can, holding it before throwing the rear wheel sideways. This is where the trick will look either really good or really lame. Holding it for a long time looks stylish and adds a degree of difficulty to the Whip. Once I'm at peak height, I spot the landing ramp, stick my head over the front end of my bike, and yank on the bars to pull the bike around. This starts to straighten me out and in turn whips the rear wheel around in a gyroscopic motion."

"As the tail end swings out, I try to keep my body in a straight angle with my shoulders pointing to the spot I want to land at. I use my legs to let the bike go sideways, but with my head and body pointing toward the landing, I know I will stick it."

"Toward the end of the trick, I start to use my legs to bring the bike back to a normal position. Basically, you want to squeeze your legs together on the bike, putting the most force on the leg that is on the side of the bike being thrown sideways. Keep your eyes on the landing ramp, and hopefully by this point you've left yourself enough airtime to get the bike back to a straight position. Hold tight as you hit the landing ramp. Make sure you are standing up, allowing your knees and elbows to absorb the impact of the landing."

A couple of years ago, the Hart Attack was one of the toughest tricks out there. In fact, at the time when the original *Freestyle Motocross: Jump Tricks from the Pros* was published, only two riders could pull off this trick. With the progression of the sport, nearly every rider at a contest can pull a Hart Attack. Realizing this, freestyle ace Tommy Clowers took the trick to the next level by adding the "Look Back."

The **Hart Attack Look Back** is one of several tricks that have been based on the Superman Seat Grab, which Hart also brought to the sport. The setup of the three tricks is very similar, but the main difference between them is that with the Hart Attack, the rider extends himself vertically behind the bike, and with the Hart Attack Look Back the rider gets vertical and at the same time points his head back and looks directly behind him. The closer to straight up and down the rider is when he is behind the rear fender, the more impressive the trick is, and riders who throw the trick to its fullest potential often feel their helmet's mouthpiece scraping their chest!

Just like nearly every freestyle trick, the Look Back has evolved even further, and riders are now able to do double seat grabs while in the same position. The Hart Attack Look Back is an extremely difficult trick because the rider can become disoriented in the air while looking back. Tommy shows us how to do it here at Fudge's house in San Diego County, and he recommends that you have a jump that is at least 80 feet long to try the trick, although it can be done on smaller jumps once perfected.

Tommy Clowers
Philadelphia, PA

Tommy Clowers explains the
HART ATTACK LOOK BACK

1 "The Hart Attack Look Back is a pretty difficult trick, so be really careful when trying it. You need a pretty decent-sized jump to practice it on so that you will have plenty of time to extend the move out fully and still make it back on to your bike safely. You can see from this photo that I start the Hart Attack Look Back immediately after I get into the air. Within a foot or two of being off of the lip, I am already bringing my left hand back toward the rear grab handle that I have cut out in my left number plate."

2 "In this second photo, my hand has made contact with the grab handle, which is an important first step. The next part of the trick is to begin to bring your legs back to the rear end of the bike. My left leg naturally goes back a little before my right leg because of the fact that I am grabbing with my left side, but this is OK. You can still see that my right leg is coming off of the footpeg, and I have plenty of time to get it back to the rear of the bike."

3 "By now, both feet are up off of the pegs and making their way back to the rear end, and up to this point the trick still looks like a Superman Seat Grab. I have a firm grip on the motorcycle with both hands, my right hand on the grip and my left hand on the grab handle. The main thing that I am concentrating on at this point is bringing my legs back, and I also double-check the balance of the bike. I want to make sure that the bike is stable in the air before I go upside down!"

4 "Here I am continuing the extension, and my legs are making their way up toward the sky. I have already gone past the point of a standard Superman Seat Grab. One thing you want to double-check here is that the bike is stable up to this point. You don't want to be front-end high, or low for that matter, because once you extend your legs way up, there is not much you can do to make corrections to it."

"In this fifth photo, I am nearing full extension of the Hart Attack. The bike is still nice and stable, with the front end just slightly higher than the rear. This is the position that you want your motorcycle to be in. Even though my legs and body are almost upside down by now, notice that my head is looking straight back, completely behind me. It is important to get your head back and hold it there for as long as possible, because this is what you get scored on."

"In this frame, I am coming down from full extension. To do this, you can't just rely on gravity to pull you down. You have to pull yourself down with both hands. You will notice that my handlebars are turning to the right, and there is a reason for this. The bars are turning because of the fact that I am pulling down with my right hand. This is all right; it can be fixed later."

"I am still coming down from the Hart Attack, and my handlebars and front end are continuing to turn. There is plenty of time and height left, but I want to get back to a normal position on the bike as soon as possible. I will keep my hand on the grab handle a little longer, until my legs get down farther toward the footpegs."

"In this eighth and final photo, I have released my left hand from the side grab handle and brought it up to the grip. This will help straighten out the bars before touching down, as you can see from the photo. My legs are inches from the pegs, and I only have about five feet until I land. Once I am back into a proper position on the bike, I will continue standing up to brace for the shock of landing."

SHAOLIN
BAR HOP

The **Shaolin Bar Hop** is a fairly new trick that was derived from an old one. Back in 1997, 6-foot 4-inch freestyle giant Shawn Highland brought the original version of the Bar Hop to the freestyle scene while filming for the first Moto XXX video on a huge step-up jump. With the original version, riders raise both feet up and over the handlebars, stick them straight out over the front fender, and then bring them back over the bars before returning to the footpegs. The Bar Hop is a relatively difficult trick due to the chance that the riders' feet can catch on the bars while coming down from the move.

At an Air MX Challenge in Bakersfield, California, in 2000, Ronnie Faisst took the Bar Hop to the next level by kicking his legs out in a full "spread eagle" position at peak extension. The leg movement not only adds a substantial amount of difficulty to the trick, but it also looks a lot better and gets more cheers from the crowd. Named after the fiercest form of Buddhist martial art monks, the Shaolin has become an extremely popular trick in recent contests.

To attempt the Shaolin, Faisst suggests that riders have their jumps set at a minimum of 80 feet apart to allow for full extension of the trick. On the subsequent pages, the originator himself performs his Shaolin at the Mulisha Compound in Temecula, California, on a jump that is set at about 85 feet.

Dan Pastor

Philadelphia, PA

Ronnie Faisst explains the
SHAOLIN BAR HOP

"The Shaolin Bar Hop is a pretty gnarly trick. Even though you're over the top of the bike and you can pretty much see what's going on, it's one of the toughest tricks because it's hard to get both feet up, over, and through the handlebars, and at the same time spread them out so far at the peak. I approached this jump in third gear, with my body in a neutral, "attack" position and my head looking forward."

"Almost immediately after I launch off of the lip, about three or four feet into the air, I bring my knees up to my chest absolutely as far as possible. You have to almost exaggerate the movement to make sure that you clear your bars, and if you don't, you're in trouble. I sometimes bring my knees so far up that I actually hit my helmet with my knee guards."

"At mid-flight extension, I do a double front kick through my handlebars. This trick requires a lot of flexibility, and to make it look its best, you should try to kick your legs out as straight as possible. Also, make sure that you're holding on tight to the grips in the air, because there's a chance that the force of your legs kicking out against your arms can knock your hands off the bars."

"After I'm past the midpoint in my flight, I begin to bring the trick down by again pulling in my knees toward my chest. I keep my head very high to allow even more clearance for my legs, and I make sure that they're bent enough before I try to clear the bars."

"Now that I know my knees are bent far enough, I start to pull them down over the handlebars. This is probably the most nerve-wracking moment of the trick. As you can see from the sequence, I have my knees bent as far as they will go, and I'm still only clearing the top of my Pro Tapers by an inch or two."

6 "Once you know that your boots have made it completely over the bars, the trick is pretty much downhill from there. All you have to remember to do now is separate your feet to get them over the gas tank and seat, and begin to descend them toward your pegs."

7 "At this point, I've separated my boots and legs, and I have just about brought them down far enough to touch the pegs. Even before they make contact, though, I am already gripping the sides of the bike's frame with the inside of my legs. This really helps to brace you for the landing, and also keeps the bike stable."

From the crowd's perspective, the **Nothing** has to be one of the scariest-looking tricks out there. During the Nothing, the rider leaves the bike completely while in the air, and for a brief moment is making no contact whatsoever with the bike's handlebars or footpegs, leaving him floating through the air in a state of apparent complete weightlessness.

Who pulled the first Nothing on a motocross bike is unclear, but explaining how the trick came to be is pretty simple. The Nothing is basically just a combination of the no-hander and the no-footer, tricks that have been pulled on BMX bikes for years. This is one of the tricks that was made popular by the best freestyler in the world, Travis Pastrana, while he was still on 80-cc machines

in the mid to late 1990s.

The Nothing takes advantage of the laws of gravity and the principle that everything that goes up must come down. The rider floats off of his bike in midair, but catches up with it before it hits the ground. While up there, the rider extends both his legs and his arms to their fullest and straightest extent, holds them there as long as possible, and then grabs the bike and lands.

The Nothing doesn't really require too long a jump, but instead requires a fairly steep lip that pops the rider up into the air instead of throwing him out far and fast. Jeff Tilton performs the jump in the following sequence over an 80-foot gap in San Diego County, but says that it can be done on jumps set at only 50 feet apart.

Luke Urek
Philadelphia, PA

Jeff Tilton explains the
NOTHING

1 "Nothings are one of the best-feeling tricks out there, but at the same time they are a little bit sketchy due to the odd feeling of weightlessness and floating that you get in the air, when you are completely away from your bike and hanging there just above it. I always make sure that the lip has a good steep pitch to it before attempting this move, because you need to be popped straight up in the air for the trick to work, making sure that the bike is not going out away from the jump faster than it is going up toward the sky."

2 "As I left the lip of the ramp, the first thing I was making sure of was that my bike was launching up in the air completely level and my weight was distributed evenly over the bike. If at this point you feel that the bike is starting to go nose high or into an endo, you need to forget about doing the trick this time and save it for another jump, because you will get hurt."

"I'm confident that my bike is nice and level at this point, so I begin the Nothing. First I remove my feet from the pegs and begin kicking my legs out and away from the bike, toward the sides. Although the photo doesn't show me releasing my hands and arms just yet, it is literally a fraction of a second after this that I begin to stick my arms out to the sides too."

"Here, I am pictured bringing both my arms and both my legs out and completely away from the bike. I try to do this as smoothly and evenly as possible because it makes the trick look way better if your arms and legs are perfectly coordinated and leaving the bike simultaneously."

"This is peak extension on the Nothing. My arms and legs are spread out and away from the bike equally, and except for a small area on my butt, I am completely detached from the motorcycle in midair, making it a Nothing. Hold the trick out there as long as possible to make it look stylish, but be careful that the bike doesn't start its motion downward before you grab ahold of it, or you can get yourself into big trouble. Notice how straight, level, and even my bike is. The rear wheel is just barely below the front wheel, the perfect position for hopping back onto the motorcycle."

"I am now beginning my downward descent, and because of that I start to bring my arms and legs back onto the motorcycle. Again, I try to stay nice and symmetrical here, with both sides of my body coming down equally and at the same time as the other. I was sure to not distance myself too far from the seat during the trick's peak extension, and that helped guarantee my safe landing. The bike floated up into me on its ascent, so I made sure to catch it while it was leveling up and before it started dropping down."

"I'm just about back onto my bike and in control now. I try to bring my arms and legs back to the bike at roughly the same time, but of course it's most important to grab the bars first because your legs can always find the pegs when you get closer to the ground, but your arms need to get ahold of the bars quickly."

"Now that I have my feet back on the pegs and my hands back on the bars, I feel like I am once again in control and cruising, but the trick is not over yet—I still have to land safely and ride away from it. You can see that I am still in a sitting position on the bike, and if I land like that it's going to hurt!"

"As you get closer to landing time, move your butt off the seat slightly to brace for the impact. I allow the nose of my bike to drop slightly so that I hit the landing ramp smooth and level. I also keep my elbows and knees slightly bent."

ONE-HANDED
SEAT GRAB

When freestyle pioneer Carey Hart pulled the first Superman Seat Grab several years ago, expanding Jeremy McGrath's Superman by adding a grab, it's safe to say that even Hart himself didn't know what kind of an impact the move would have on freestyle. This single trick probably has more variations than any other, and it has been a catalyst for crowd appreciation of the sport.

One of the most entertaining of all is the **One-Handed Seat Grab**, a trick that thrills fans because, at peak extension, the rider is hanging on to his nearly-250-pound bike by only five fingers. At the beginning of the trick, it looks like the rider is just throwing a standard Superman Seat Grab, but once he has enough altitude, he drops his hand off of the handlebars and pulls it back behind him, near his feet. An extremely difficult maneuver, the One-Handed Seat Grab is one of the most dangerous variations of Hart's original trick. Although there are quite a few pros now doing this trick, the first rider to do it at an organized contest was Travis Pastrana, who threw the move at the 2000 Summer X Games in San Francisco, California.

Performing the One-Handed Seat Grab in the following sequence is Metal Mulisha General Brian Deegan. The jump that Deegan is on is about 85 feet long, which Brian says is just about the right size for the trick. You'll notice that Deegan is also adding an Indian Air on this particular jump, something that is done to add more style to Brian's One-Handed Seat Grab.

Jake Windham
Philadelphia, PA

Brian Deegan explains the
ONE-HANDED SEAT GRAB

1 "One-Handed Seat Grabs are pretty good point-gaining tricks that also look really good, but they are tough. Learn your Superman Seat Grabs well first, and then make sure you feel comfortable letting go of the bike in the air. To learn this feeling, you might want to try doing some Nothings so you feel at ease being away from the bike. For this trick the bigger the jump the better for extension. If you have a big enough jump, the trick looks really smooth and you will feel like you are floating behind your bike. Just don't let go!"

2 "I approach the ramp just like I would for a regular Superman Seat Grab. I stay centered on the bike, standing up and crouching slightly as I hit the transition. Here I'm in third gear, right in the middle of the powerband. As soon as I launch my bike into the air, I make sure that the wheels are fairly level, and if anything I want the nose down slightly because when I grab the seat, it'll pull the back fender down a little. If you're already nose high when this happens, you can get into trouble if your back end drops too much."

3 "Once I'm comfortable with the bike's position in the air, I start to throw the trick. I start the trick like I do a Superman Seat Grab. I pull my left hand off of the handlebars and reach back to find the grab hole in my number plate, while at the same time taking my feet off of the footpegs and throwing them back toward the rear of the bike."

4 "Right around the time my chest is lined up with the back fender, I start to remove my other hand from its grip on the bars. Of course, I make sure that my other hand has a firm grasp on the grab handle and the seat before letting my other hand come off. The earlier you can remove both hands from the bars the better, just make sure you always have some kind of contact with the bike. You can see in the picture that once I have let go, I immediately bring my hand back and up in the air. This shows the crowd and judges that my hand is completely off of the bike and looks better than just letting your arm hang there."

"In this jump, I decided to throw in an Indian Air to add some style to the One-Handed Seat Grab. This is something I started doing after I learned the trick and could do it easily, so wait until you have the move down before throwing in variations. While at peak extension, I concentrate on making sure that I am as far off of the bike as possible. The more you separate yourself from the bike, the cleaner the trick will look. Obviously, though, you can't go too far, or you risk not being able to get back on the bike."

6 "Once you have held it for as long as you possibly can, you need to get back toward the front of the bike and gain control. To do this, pull hard on the seat with whichever hand is holding on to the bike. This will get you forward where you need to be. Bring your floating hand back to its place on the bars. The second you feel contact with the grip, grab hard and bring your seat-grabbing hand and both feet back to their positions on the bike."

7 "If you held it long enough, you'll have just enough time to get back on the bike comfortably before touching down. Keep your knees and elbows bent and your head forward, spotting the landing."

The **Whipped Double Nac Nac** is a fairly new trick that takes the standard Nac Nac to another level. The original Nac Nac has a very important history in the sport of freestyle motocross. Jeremy McGrath made this maneuver his signature victory celebration trick, and performed Nac Nacs on the final laps of his winning races in stadiums around the world. What made this so important to freestyle motocross was that the move brought the underground sport to fans everywhere.

The Whipped Double Nac Nac is just an extension of the original, but the difference is that the rider kicks both legs out to the side of the bike instead of just one leg, and at the same time throws the bike sideways into a classic whip. During the best Whipped Double Nac Nacs, the rider will extend both legs out and straighten them, with the bike completely sideways.

Metal Mulisha General Brian Deegan performed the first Double Nac Nacs at his compound several years ago. At the time, the trick was really experimental, and Brian only tried it a few times before crashing and deciding to wait for a while before attempting another one. Not too long after that, Mike Metzger became the first rider to try the trick at a contest. Now, several riders have perfected it, and variations have been added to the trick, including the Cat Nac or Mulisha March, in which the rider moves his feet in a walking motion next to the bike.

Showing us the proper technique of the Whipped Double Nac Nac is freestyle rider "Mad" Mike Jones, who performs the trick at Manny's Jump Park in Lake Elsinore, California. Jones can perform the trick on jumps as small as 70 feet apart, but prefers an 85-foot-long hit to really throw the trick properly.

Tommy Clowers
San Jacinto, CA

WHIPPED DOUBLE NAC NAC

Mike Jones explains the
WHIPPED DOUBLE NAC NAC

1 "Whipped Double Nac Nacs are probably one of the coolest-feeling tricks that I have learned lately, and they really aren't that hard to do. They feel cool, because you're whipping out your bike and at the same time taking your legs off and floating behind the bike. I approach this hit, which is about 85 feet long, in third gear about mid-throttle. I actually lean the bike over on the face of the jump slightly as if I'm going for a mellow whip. You can see that my body is leaning slightly to the side."

2 "From here, I have set up for a Whip and am throwing the bike sideways. I am still gaining altitude and I need to get the bike a little more sideways before extending the trick, but I have already started the first part of the Nac Nac. My boot comes off of the right footpeg as I am starting to throw it over the bike like I would have done for a normal Nac Nac. You can't waste any time with this trick, because you need plenty of time at the end of the trick to get your feet back on the pegs."

3 "Now I've got the bike pretty much sideways, so I will start to prepare for the trick by extending my right leg over the rear fender while beginning to remove my left leg from its peg. Although the photo might not show it, I don't remove my legs in one motion. Instead, I take off my right leg slightly earlier, then I pull off my left leg a little later."

4 "I am now fully committed to the Whipped Double Nac Nac, and both of my legs are starting to kick out behind me. If you look closely, you'll notice that my head and body are both starting to turn slightly to the right. This helps me get my leg over the seat and turn far enough over to make the trick look good."

5 "Once I am at full extension of the trick, I allow my head and body to get twisted slightly to the right, and this helps me tweak out the Whipped Double Nac Nac to its fullest extent. Another hint to help extend Double Nac Nacs even further is to concentrate on throwing both legs into a full back kick off of the rear left side of the bike, instead of just barely hanging your legs off to the side. It looks a lot better when done this way."

6 "As I'm coming down from the peak of the jump, I need to start bringing the trick back. The easiest way to do this is to pretend that you are getting on your bike when you're on the ground, and swing your leg over the seat. Make sure that you get your boot well over the seat, because if you get your boot caught, you're in trouble! You don't have to worry too much about your other leg, as it will find the peg pretty naturally. Instead, concentrate on getting the right leg over the seat."

"Again, make sure that your boot is going to clear the saddle, and at the same time swing your head and body all the way to the left. Remember, where your head goes, your body follows. Start to spot the landing, and get both feet back on the pegs as quickly as possible."

"Toward the end of the sequence, I've spotted my landing, and I'm coming down a little nose-first. This is natural because of the sideways motion that you do when executing the Whipped Double Nac Nac. Just make sure that you are standing up, ready to brace yourself for the landing."

CAT NAC

Tommy Clowers' radical **Cat Nac** is one of the many tricks that have helped the Tomcat establish himself as not only one of the top riders on the circuit but also one of the most inventive. The Cat Nac is one of many variations that have been added to the Double Nac Nac, and like most of them, the move consists of many parts that combine to create a whole. The trick is basically a culmination of the Whip, Double Nac, and Indian Air, but when the rider is fully extended at the pinnacle of the move, his body is slightly inverted and twisted sideways.

Performing the Cat Nac is far from easy, and before attempting the trick riders should feel completely comfortable pulling tricks like the Double Nac Nac and any of the several different Indian Air variations, where the legs are kicked out sideways and over each other. Once these tricks have become effortless for the rider, performing the Cat Nac is as easy as adding the Indian Air portion more and more each time until it becomes second nature and allows for full extension of the trick.

As is the case with most riders, Tommy likes to have a long gap to jump so that he can tweak the trick as far as possible, but when forced to jump on smaller jumps in arenas, Clowers can still pull the trick on 65-foot hits. He does it in the following sequence on an 80-foot-long ramp-to-dirt jump in San Diego County.

CAT NAC

Travis Pastrana
Philadelphia, PA

Tommy Clowers explains the
CAT NAC

1 "The Cat Nac is probably my favorite trick right now, because I love the feeling of whipping the bike sideways while extending and twisting my body out to the opposite side. I start the trick by preparing for a whip as I leave the ramp, turning the bike slightly and also leaning to the side a little. As usual, I am standing in a somewhat crouched position as I take off."

2 "Once in the air, I waste no time in throwing the trick. This allows me to tweak the Cat Nac more at the peak of my height. In one big swinging motion, I throw the bike into its whip as I bring my right leg over the top of the seat and rear fender, just as if I were doing a Nac Nac. In this photo, you can see that right about the point where my right leg has gotten past the seat, I begin to pull my left foot off the peg. I am continuing the sideways whip, but before throwing my legs completely out to the side, I have made certain that I have the speed to clear the jump comfortably and safely."

"Although this is fairly early in the jump, my lower torso is already completely detached from the motorcycle. The rear end of the bike is continuing to swing around, and I am basically doing a standard Double Nac Nac."

"As I get further away from the bike, the trick is starting to take form. I am swinging my legs around and preparing them to face the opposite side of my motorcycle. Notice how my right leg is on its way upward—at the peak of the Cat Nac, it will be in front of my left leg in the Indian Air position."

"Here I am at peak extension. My body is twisted completely sideways, and I'm throwing the classic Indian Air position with my legs. Note that I keep my head looking forward and down, toward the landing. This helps me from going too far and getting in trouble. If you have your eyes on the landing, you're pretty much guaranteed to pull the trick cleanly."

"Now I'm starting to come down from my Cat Nac, and the first step in doing this is to release the Indian Air portion and start to straighten your feet. My bike is still really whipped at this point, but that is okay—it will straighten itself out. Your main worry should be getting your feet back on the pegs."

"As the bike starts to straighten itself out, I am preparing to get my feet back to their original positions, most importantly concentrating on getting my right leg over the seat without catching up on anything. You want to be pretty far forward to minimize any chance of getting your boot caught on the seat."

"My bike is now pretty straight, and my left foot is only inches from the peg. My right foot is still pretty high, but it's on its way down. Notice how far above the seat my boot is. Again, this is just to ensure I don't hit the seat with my boot."

"Just a few feet from landing, my bike is perfectly straight and I am in a good position to hit the dirt landing. Although my right leg still isn't in contact with the foot peg, it is only a few inches from being there, which is okay. It will instinctively fall back on right before I land."

INDIAN AIR
DOUBLE
SEAT GRAB

The **Indian Air Double Seat Grab** is one of the hardest new tricks out there, but when performed successfully it draws some of the biggest roars from the crowd. Like many of the new moves in this book, the Indian Air Double Seat Grab is a highly evolved trick that combines several older tricks into one huge move that is simply amazing to witness.

Way back in the beginning days of freestyle motocross, Jeremy McGrath first did the Superman, which we can trace as the first step in creating the Indian Air Double Seat Grab. From there, Carey Hart added the seat grab to further the Superman's progress and make the trick even more difficult. Next came the Indian Air Seat Grab, a trick where the rider does a scissors kick behind the bike while holding onto a cutout in the rear number plate. Add to all of this the Double Seat Grab, where the rider lets go of the handlebars and grabs cutouts in the rear number plates on both sides of the bike, mix them together, and you have the Indian Air Double Seat Grab.

The reason that this trick is so difficult is that there is so much going on while the rider is performing the move. Letting go of the handlebars and getting behind the bike, stretching out the legs, and then getting back on the bike and locating the handlebars again are all required to pull the Indian Air Double Seat Grab.

Pulling the Indian Air Double Seat Grab in the following sequence is Trevor Vines, jumping at the dairy farms of Norco, California. This jump was set at a gap of about 80 feet, which is the minimum distance that Vines recommends for learning the move to ensure adequate air time.

Brian Deegan
Temecula, CA

INDIAN AIR DOUBLE SEAT GRAB

Trevor Vines explains the
INDIAN AIR DOUBLE SEAT GRAB

1 "This trick is pretty difficult, so make sure that you are doing your regular Double Seat Grabs and Indian Air Seat Grabs relatively easily before attempting the move. I approach the takeoff for the Indian Air Double Seat Grab very similarly to the way that I do for the other Superman Seat Grab tricks I do. Immediately off of the lip, just a few feet into the air, I am already beginning to bring my left hand back by taking it off of the bars and finding the grab handle I have cut into my number plate. I pull the left hand off first because I feel most comfortable using that hand on my grabs."

2 "I always wait until I have a nice, firm grasp on my left-hand side grab handle that is cut into my number plate before doing anything else. Once I feel that I have a good hold onto the frame, the next step in the trick is to remove both of your feet from the footpegs. With my feet off the pegs, I start to bring my legs back toward the rear fender."

3 "Once I have both feet off the pegs and toward the rear of the motorcycle, I begin to bring my entire body back with them. When I have gotten my weight back there, I remove my right hand and find the other grab handle. I haven't gotten into the horizontal Superman Seat Grab position just yet, as I am still gaining altitude and bringing my body back. My head is in an upward, forward position, and I am double-checking to make sure that I will clear the jump before I fully commit to doing the trick."

4 "This is the point where I would normally throw my legs straight back for a Double Seat Grab, but since I am doing the Indian Air variation, I start to turn my body to the left. This should be done by turning the hips first, which will allow the rest of your body to twist around accordingly."

5 "At the peak of the jump, I fully extend the trick by doing a full-on scissors kick behind the motorcycle. You can see in the sequence that my hips are twisted completely to the left, at a 90-degree angle to the ground. This is where the Indian Air really comes in, and you can see how much different the trick looks compared to a regular Double Seat Grab."

6 "After throwing out the trick as far as I can, I begin my descent back down toward the ground. To start this portion, the first thing you need to do is stabilize your body, bringing it back to a normal, horizontal position on the bike. Once you are straightened out and you feel comfortable with the way your body is suspended, you can start to bring the trick back to a normal position."

7 "In one swift move, I am throwing my body weight up to the front of the bike. I do this by taking my right hand off of the grab handle first, which automatically returns to the grip. At the same time, I bring my legs and feet up toward the footpegs and pull my weight up to the front, using the boost I received from pulling hard on the grab handle. I leave my left hand on a bit longer than my right, again because I am more comfortable grabbing with the left side, and I don't want to be in the air completely detached from the motorcycle."

8 "Both hands come in contact with both grips before my feet touch the pegs, because grabbing with your hands is more important for gaining control than having your feet on the pegs. Once my hands and legs are back on and I am comfortable on the bike, I am basically in cruise control. I have also spotted my landing, and I know that I have plenty of time to straighten out the front end and prepare myself for landing. As with any trick, you want to land smoothly. To do this, keep standing and use your legs and elbows as shock absorbers."

INDIAN AIR
BAR HOP

The Bar Hop is currently one of the most popular tricks on the freestyle contest circuit. There are several variations of the original trick, which was first performed by Shawn Highland in 1997, in the early days of freestyle motocross. In the original, the rider thrusts his legs up and over the handlebars, extends them way out over the front of the bike, and eventually brings them back down over the handlebars.

We've already looked at one of the more established new versions of the trick, the Shaolin Bar Hop, a trick that martial artist Ronnie Faisst brought to the sport. The **Indian Air Bar Hop** is actually very similar to the Shaolin, but the difference is in the positioning of the legs. With the Shaolin Bar Hop, the rider extends his legs out to the "spread eagle" position on the bike, stretching them out as far as possible before bringing them back over the top of the handlebars and returning them to the side of the bike. With the Indian Air version, instead of spreading his legs apart, the rider does just the opposite. Once the legs are over the handlebars, the rider crosses them over each other, just as he would do when performing an Indian Air Seat Grab.

Bar Hop guru Ronnie Faisst was again the first to pull this variation of the original trick. Faisst actually doesn't even do the trick that often in contests, as he favors the look of the Shaolin, which he invented after the Indian Air version. Still, Ronnie does occasionally bust the trick out, and every time he does, the crowd eats it up. Faisst performs the trick at the Mulisha Compound in Temecula, California.

Ronnie Faisst
Temecula, CA

Ronnie Faisst explains the
INDIAN AIR BAR HOP

1 "The Indian Air Bar Hop is basically just a spin-off of the Shaolin Bar Hop, but instead of spreading my legs out, I cross them over each other. I always like to do the trick on at least a 70-foot jump, but of course prefer a longer gap so that I can hold it and make the move look better. This jump is about 85 feet, which is adequate. In the first shot, I am thinking about hitting the lip perfectly straight, centered, and staying comfortable on the bike. I am also standing up and looking straight ahead, preparing to launch into the air."

2 "In the second picture, I'm staying balanced on my bike, with my upper torso up near my handlebars. I am already throwing my legs up and over the handlebars, making sure that I clear them with both of my heels. You can't wait very long on any form of Bar Hop to bring your legs over the bars. If you do, you may wind up with inadequate time to get your feet back over at the end, which will cause you to go down hard."

"By this point, I am already raising my legs up pretty high, and I've cleared the triple clamps and handlebars with no problem whatsoever. The minute I get my legs over the bars, I immediately begin the Indian Air portion of the trick. You don't want to wait for until you get into a Bar Hop position first before throwing the Indian Air, because you won't have time to extend it properly."

"In the fourth picture, I am pretty well into the position that I want to be. I have my legs crossing one another, with my left leg over my right leg. Once they are crossed over like this, I just try to concentrate on bringing the left leg as far to the right as possible, and vice versa."

"In this shot, I am pretty much at the peak extension of the Indian Air Bar Hop. Once I feel that I have reached the full extension, I try to hold it there. This trick can be held fairly long, depending on how quick you throw it, but just make sure you get back on the bike with plenty of time to spare. Remember, it's pretty easy to hang your feet up on the bars if you're not careful, so don't hold it for too long. Although this photo looks a lot like the last one, the biggest difference is that in this one I've thrust my hips out toward the front fender to make it look better."

6 "Here I am centered over the bike with my feet coming back over the handlebars. As I said in the earlier captions, you have to really be careful not to catch your feet here. To prevent this, I almost exaggerate my knees going toward my chest, clearing my bars by a good few inches. This will feel more and more natural with every time you do the trick, and after a while you begin to become accustomed to the feeling of the Bar Hop.

7 "I'm in the clear zone now, because my boots are over the crossbar with plenty of time left in the air to regain my composure on the bike. The only thing you really need to be concerned with at this point is making sure that you remember to spread your legs out enough to get them over the seat. If they are too close, you can catch the seat with your boot tips, which is almost as bad as catching the bars."

8 "As I make my way back down from the trick, I've almost found my footpegs, which is a good thing considering how quickly I'm coming back down to earth. This will come easily once your feet have made it past the seat, so now you should be thinking about spotting your landing."

9 "In this final frame, I have both of my feet back to their regular position over the pegs. My head is forward and I'm balanced over the center of the bike, with my shoulders, elbows, and knees absorbing the landing. If I have time, I even try to squeeze the bike with my boots to brace myself a little more for the landing."

DOUBLE
NAC NAC
REVERSE
INDIAN AIR

Trick combos are getting longer and more advanced in freestyle motocross with every contest, and the **Double Nac Nac Reverse Indian Air** is clear evidence of this progression. This trick merges several different moves into one big amalgamation that, when thrown correctly, looks every bit as buttery smooth as a regular Double Nac Nac.

When Brian Deegan first did the trick in 2000, his objective was to take an existing trick and reverse the moves. The trick Deegan selected for modification was the Cat Nac, a move that Tommy Clowers came up with that involves the rider crossing his legs in the Indian Air position at the peak extension of his Double Nac Nac, when he is farthest away from the bike. Deegan does the exact opposite when he maxes out his Double Nac: instead of throwing his legs out to the side opposite his seat and away from the bike, he twists his body the other way, toward his bike, performing the Indian Air over his seat.

Brian is performing his signature trick on an 85-foot-long ramp-to-dirt hit at the Metal Mulisha Compound in Temecula, California. The Double Nac Nac Reverse Indian Air can be performed on a smaller jump than this, probably on a gap as small as 60 feet, but for good extension Deegan likes a nice long jump with a steep ramp face to kick him high into the air. Before you try this trick, Brian advises that you learn regular Double Nac Nacs as well as some sort of trick with an Indian Air variation in it so that you get the feeling of crossing your legs over one another in the air.

Travis Pastrana
Philadelphia, PA

Brian Deegan explains the
DOUBLE NAC NAC REVERSE INDIAN AIR

1 "The Double Nac Nac Reverse Indian Air is basically just an extension of a standard Double Nac Nac, but just takes it to a further extreme. As in the regular trick, you wind up whipping your bike sideways as you take both feet off of the pegs and extend them both to one side of the bike, pulling a leg over the rear fender. The biggest difference is that with this variation, you wind up over the top of the bike more, with your legs crossed. To start the trick, I leave the lip slightly sideways like I do when I am whipping the bike, carving an arc up the face of the jump."

2 "I tend to throw this trick pretty late, so I let the bike get nice and whipped before I even begin to take my legs off. Once I feel that the bike is sufficiently sideways and I have some good, lofty hang time, I begin to remove my feet from the footpegs."

"I start with the right leg, which is the leg that sits on the side of the bike that I am whipping it toward. Just as if I am doing a regular Nac Nac, I bring my leg up and over the top of the seat and rear fender. At the same time, my other foot is also coming off of its peg and is rising slightly in preparation for the Indian Air."

"I am now twisting my whole body to the side. I start the twisting with my hips and legs, and continue on by turning my shoulders and head slightly. Even though my head isn't turned that far, turning it like I'm doing here is a very important step in doing the trick well because it makes you kick out sideways and tweak your legs more."

"I try to plan the trick so that when the bike is whipped the most, I am at the peak extension of my Indian Air. When you find yourself in this position, hold it here as long as possible before straightening the bike back out and putting your feet on the pegs." "When I'm at my full extension, you can see just how different this trick is compared to a regular Double Nac Nac or a Cat Nac. My legs are completely inverted, and I am looking to the side of the bike."

"When you feel like you've held the trick long enough, coming down is fairly easy. Just let the bike begin to naturally straighten itself from the whip, while at the same time separating your legs and letting them go to their respective sides of the bike."

I try to get both of my feet back on to the pegs while I still have at least ten feet of hang time left so that I will have enough time to regain composure and brace myself for hitting the landing. In this sequence, you can see that I have plenty of time to remount the bike and straighten it out, all of which ensures a nice smooth touchdown."

Similar to the Double Nac Nac and the Whipped Double Nac Nac, the scissored version adds a leg kick in the middle of the trick to heighten the difficulty, making it look even better than the original versions.

The **Scissored Double Nac Nac** has its roots with the Double Nac Nac, which Mike Metzger first did in competition in 2000, at a jump show in Austria. At the time, Mike Jones, who takes credit for adding the Scissors kick, thought Metzger was getting ready to throw away the bike in midair! Jonesy had never seen the trick before and was watching from the sidelines when Metzger debuted the move, where he separates his entire body, except for his hands, from the bike.

Fast forward one year, and Mad Mike is now a master of the Double Nac. In fact, Jones has such confidence in his ability to do the trick that adding variations just came naturally. Jones has been seen doing the Scissored Double Nac Nac at a variety of locations, and he'll even throw it off natural terrain jumps.

As with most of the tricks he does, Jones prefers a fairly sizable gap to do the Scissored Double Nac Nac because of all of the extension and movement required to perform the trick correctly. He also recommends that you learn both Double Nac Nacs and Whipped Double Nac Nacs before attempting the scissored version.

Mike Jones
Philadelphia, PA

Mike Jones explains the
SCISSORED DOUBLE NAC NAC

1 "I like to find a big jump to do my Scissored Double Nac Nacs on so that I can throw them out nice and fat, but they can be done on smaller jumps. This jump, at Manny's Yard in Lake Elsinore, California, is about 85 feet long, which is just about the perfect gap for the trick. I start the jump as I would start any jump, with plenty of speed and in a regular body position, standing up with my elbows and head up."

2 "About five feet out from the take off, I start to throw the trick. My body is still in an upright position on the bike, but now you can see that I have just started to bring my right leg up and over the seat, just like I would if I were performing a standard Nac Nac. Notice that at this point, which is not very far off the jump, I have not yet lifted my left leg. I like to wait until my right leg is over the bike before I pull my other leg off."

3 "Now I am probably about ten feet off of the lip; I know that I must start acting quickly so that I will have enough time to pull the trick. Both legs are off of the bike now, and this picture was taken just before I begin the scissors kick. Obviously, you need to get into the Double Nac position before kicking your legs."

4 "This photo shows me at my peak extension of the trick. Note how far my legs are kicked out. The farther you separate and kick them, the cooler your Scissored Double Nac Nac will look. Another important part of the trick to note here is how far up on the bike I am. My head is above the handlebars, as I have pulled the bars toward my chest fairly hard with my arms. The cool part about this trick is that your right leg ends up way over on the opposite side, to the left of your body."

5 "I held the trick as long as I possibly could to add some style to it, but eventually you need to bring the scissors kick back down and get your feet onto the footpegs. To do this, continue to keep your weight way up toward the front end and think about getting your right leg back over the seat. You need to be most concerned about your right leg, because your left leg will find the peg pretty naturally."

6 "As I continue to come down from the Scissored Double Nac Nac, I am still concerned with getting my right leg over the bike. Because I'm concerned about clearing the seat and avoiding a hang up, which could be disastrous, I bring my leg a little higher than I need to."

"My boot is now over the seat and I have plenty of hang time, so I am pretty confident that I will successfully pull the trick and land it safely. I'm still way up toward the front of the bike and ready to touch down on my footpegs."

"By now, I have regained control of the bike, and although I haven't actually made contact with my footpegs, it is only a matter of time until they naturally float back down. I have spotted my landing, and my body is in a position that will be able to take the shock of the landing without a problem. In addition, because of the Nac Nac portion of the trick, the bike was naturally whipped a little bit sideways. As soon as I touch the pegs, I will use my legs to straighten the bike out completely."

"Here, I am getting ready to touch down on the back side of the second jump. My boots have made their way down to the pegs, and I have plenty of time to regain complete control before landing. My knees and elbows are slightly bent to absorb the shock of the landing, and I am comfortable in my distance. I know that I will clear the jump, so from here I just sit back and wait to land."

BACKFLIP

Of all the tricks ever attempted in the sport of freestyle motocross, none have been as revered or elusive as the **Backflip**. Though never ridden away from, Carey Hart made history by attempting the trick at the Gravity Games in 2000 and landing on both wheels. Since then, the flip has been claimed by several, but pulled by none.

Due to the gyroscopic effect of the rear wheel and the heavy weight of a motocross bike, flips are nearly impossible on full-sized motorcycles. Who knows if and when someone will actually ride away from it first, but one thing is for sure: the flip is not for the faint of heart!

On the following pages, you'll see Carey Hart himself trying the Backflip for the second time during 2001's Summer X Games. As you'll see, the trick didn't go exactly as Carey planned . . .

BACKFLIP

Left:

Carey Hart, whipping it at Caineville.

Right:

Clifford Adoptante, Shaolin Bar Hop at
Philadelphia, PA

Dan Pastor, One-Handed Reverse Indian Air Double Nac at Philadelphia, PA

Dustin Miller, One–Handed Double Nac at Philadelphia, PA

Travis Pastrana, Whipped Cat Nac at Philadelphia, PA

Dustin Miller, Whipped Double Nac at Philadelphia, PA

Ronnie Faisst, Philadelphia, PA

Mike Jones, Kiss of Death at Caineville

Twitch, Whip at Manny's

Tommy Clowers at Ocotilla Wells

Jeff Tilton, Whip at Ocotillo Wells

Tilt, Whip at Caineville

Brain Deegan, Whip at the Mulisha Compound

Jeff Tilton, Whip at Caineville

Ryan Leyba, Whip at Glamis

Brain Deegan, Whip at the Mulisha Compound

Larry Linkogle, Whip at Caineville

Dan Pastor, Whip at Cainville

Brian Deegan, Super Can in Temecula

INDEX

Adoptante, Clifford, 109

Backflip, 102–107

Cat Nac, 72–77

Clowers, Tommy, 21, 22, 42–47, 67, 73–77, 91

DeCoster, Roger, 37

Deegan, Brian, 17, 19, 20, 61–65, 67, 79, 91–95, 118, 119, 122, 126

Double Nac Nac Reverse Indian Air, 90–95

Evans, Tyler, 17

Faisst, Ronnie, 17, 18, 49–53, 85–89

Glover, Broc, 21

Hart Attack Double Seat Grab, 30–35

Hart Attack Look Back, 42–47

Hart, Carey, 31, 61, 73, 102–108

Highland, Shawn, 49, 85

Huffman, Damon, 22

Indian Air Bar Hop, 84–89

Indian Air Double Seat Grab, 78

Johnson, Rick, 21

Jones, Mike, 18, 19, 20–23, 67, 115

Kiss of Death, 24–29, 67

Lechien, Ron, 21

Leyba, Ryan, 25, 121

Linkogle, Larry, 20, 123

McGrath, Jeremy, 31, 61, 67, 79

Metal Mulisha, 17, 18, 20, 23, 61, 67

Metzger, Mike, 16, 19, 67, 97

Miller, Dustin, 110, 112

Nothing, 54–59

One-Handed Double Nac, 110

One-Handed Reverse Indian Air Double Nac, 109

One-Handed Seat Grab, 60–65

Pastor, Dan, 37, 48, 109, 124, 125

Pastrana, Travis, 10, 14, 25, 55, 61, 73, 91, 111

Rourke, Kris, 31

Scissored Double Nac Nac, 96–101

Shaolin Bar Hop, 48–53, 109

Stenberg, Jeremy, 17, 23, 37–41, 115

Super Can, 126

Tilton, Jeff, 8, 20–22, 55–59, 116, 117, 120

Vines, Trevor, 10–17, 31–35, 79–83

Whip, 36–41, 108, 115–125

Whipped Cat Nac, 111

Whipped Double Nac Nac, 66–71, 112

Wonky Donkey, 24, 60

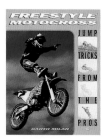

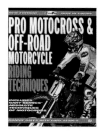
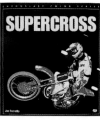
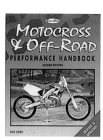